Kids' Cooking

Teddy Bears' Picnic

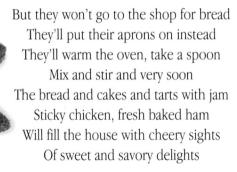

If you go down to the woods today
You'll never believe your eyes
If you go down to the woods today
You're in for a big surprise

For every bear that ever there was
Will gather there for certain because
Today's the day the Teddy Bears have their picnic...

But they won't go to the shop for bread
They'll put their aprons on instead
They'll warm the oven, take a spoon
Mix and stir and very soon
The bread and cakes and tarts with jam
Sticky chicken, fresh baked ham
Will fill the house with cheery sights
Of sweet and savory delights

With ice-cold milk and lemonade
They'll take the lovely food they've made
And on the grass amidst the trees
Their scrumptious feast is sure to please...

Adapted from the original by Liz Franklin

Kids' Cooking

Liz Franklin

p

This is a Parragon Publishing book
This edition published in 2002

Parragon Publishing
Queen Street House
4 Queen Street
Bath BA1 1HE, UK

Designed, produced, and packaged by
Stonecastle Graphics Ltd

Design by Paul Turner and Sue Pressley
Photography by Roddy Paine
Edited by Gillian Haslam

ISBN 0-75258-871-0

Printed in China

Contents

Introduction

Helping a grown-up in the kitchen is always an exciting thing to do, but can you imagine just how much more fun it might be if you're the one doing the cooking and the grown-up is simply there to help you? All those lovely ingredients to chop and stir and bake, all those little nibbles and tastes along the way, and at the end of it, a very special feeling when you proudly share your goodies with your friends or family.

Well, this book is packed with delicious recipes that are great fun to make and fabulous to eat too, from swirly pasta and simple pizzas to lip-smacking sticky-licky chicken and from fresh strawberry skewers to the chewiest chocolatey fudge that can make a perfect present for someone special with a sweet tooth.

So put on your apron, get out the pots and pans and start cooking!

Cooks' Rules

Follow these tips for keeping safe in the kitchen.

Always have an adult with you when you are cooking.

Be very careful with sharp knives.

Collect together all the ingredients that you will need before you start cooking and weigh or measure them out.

Don't open the oven door while you have things inside cooking. Food such as cakes can easily spoil if you are tempted to peep.

Floors can get very slippery if you spill anything, so if you do have an accident wipe it up straight away.

Get a special place ready with a mat or board for hot things when they come out of the oven so they don't spoil the work surface.

If you need to use the oven, always ask an adult to help you.

Use a separate chopping board if you are cutting up raw meat.

Saucepan handles should always be turned to the side, so they can't accidentally be knocked off the stove while cooking.

Always use oven gloves when handling hot food.

Wash your hands before you begin work in the kitchen and again after you have been touching raw meat.

Wear an apron and roll your sleeves up to keep your clothes clean.

Hair should be tied back if it's very long.

And don't forget about washing the dishes!

Cooks' Tools

These are very useful items to have in the kitchen. If you have a good look through the cupboards, you'll probably find that you have a lot of these things already.

Grater
Knives
Fish slice or spatula
Tin opener
Scissors
Assorted cookie cutters
Rolling pin
Sieve
Wooden spoons
Cheesecloth
Colander
Saucepans
Assorted cake pans

Baking sheets
Cooling rack
Chopping board
Mixing bowls
Measuring cups
Scales
Salt and pepper mills
Garlic press
Lemon squeezer
Food processor
Wire whisks or electric whisk
Oven gloves

Cooks' Talk

These are special words for cooks and you'll find them used in the recipes that follow.

Bake   Cook food in the oven.

Baste   Spoon the pan juices over the food during cooking to add flavor – especially when roasting and broiling.

Beat   Use a wooden spoon or whisk and lots of energy to mix ingredients together really well.

Boil   Cook food in boiling water. You can tell that water has reached boiling point when you start to see big bubbles rolling across the surface of the water together with lots of steam.

Bubble Another word for simmer.

Cream   Beat ingredients together until light and smooth (usually butter and sugar for cakes and cookies).

Fry   Cook in hot oil.

Garnish Decorate food with fresh herbs, fruit slices, chocolate curls etc, to make it look especially pretty.

Grease Use a pastry brush to paint pans and baking sheets with melted butter or vegetable oil to stop food from sticking.

Knead   Push and stretch and squeeze dough until it becomes smooth and elastic (especially bread dough).

Mash   Squash everything with a fork or potato masher until smooth (usually potatoes or other vegetables).

Pinch   Some recipes ask for a pinch of herbs. This means a sprinkle, or as much as you can hold when you pinch your thumb and finger together.

Season Add extra flavor to food using salt, pepper, herbs, or spices.

Sieve   Shake flour through a sieve to make it light or get lumps out of fine sugar or cocoa powder.

Simmer Cook a liquid over a gentle heat so that the surface just trembles but doesn't boil.

Whisk   Beat wet ingredients such as eggs or cream with a wire whisk or electric whisk to make them light.

Boiled Eggs with Granary Soldiers

Boiled eggs are brilliant for breakfast or a light tea with warm, buttery soldiers to dunk in the yolk.

For one person:

2 fresh free-range eggs

1 slice granary bread

Butter

1 Pour enough water into a medium saucepan to come halfway up the sides and bring it to the boil. Turn the heat down, so that the water simmers gently and carefully lower in the eggs using a spoon. Cook the eggs for 5 minutes.

2 Meanwhile, pop the bread into a toaster or under the broiler until cooked on both sides. Butter the toast and cut it into strips about 1/2in wide. Put the eggs into eggcups and serve at once while the toast is still hot.

Cresstop Tinkers

When you've eaten your eggs, if you save the shells and carefully wash them out, you can grow cress in them. Paint a face onto the eggshell and fill the inside with a little bit of damp absorbent cotton. Sprinkle in some cress seeds and make sure to keep the absorbent cotton slightly damp all the time. A few days later, you'll have Cresstop Tinkers – funny, eggy faces with a lovely mop of cress hair that you can cut and use in sandwiches or to decorate all sorts of food.

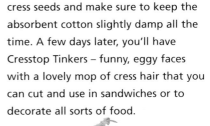

The Crunch Bunch

Meet the Crunch Bunch – crunchy, munchy toast people that are great with all kinds of lovely toppings.

For the Crunch Bunch

4 large slices white bread

4 tbsp olive oil

Pinch dried Italian herbs

Set the oven to 350°F. Always ask a grown-up to help with the oven.

1 Using a cookie cutter, cut figures out of the bread. Using a pastry brush, brush them with olive oil and sprinkle over some dried herbs. Place on a baking sheet and bake for about 5-6 minutes until golden brown.

And to put on top...

Squashy Tomatoes

Cut a tomato in half and simply rub it all over the toast. Eat it up while the toast is nice and crispy.

Tuna Spread

| 4oz tin tuna |
| $^{1}/_{2}$ cup soft cheese |
| Salt and pepper |

Stir the tuna, cheese, salt and pepper together until well mixed, then pile on top of the toast.

Egg 'n' Cress

| 2 eggs |
| 2 tbsp mayonnaise |
| Cress |
| Salt and pepper |

Follow the recipe for boiled eggs on page 10, but cook the eggs for 10 minutes. When cooked, drain them from the saucepan and then run cold water over them. When they are cold, shell them and pop them into a bowl with the mayonnaise. Squash the eggs with the back of a fork and stir everything together. Add some cress and some salt and pepper.

Creamy Tomato Soup

This is a dreamy, creamy soup full of tomato flavor. To eat with it, cheesy corn triangles make a fab change from bread – see the recipe on page 16.

For four people:

1 onion

2 tbsp olive oil

14oz tin chopped tomatoes

$1/2$ tsp superfine sugar

1 cup vegetable stock (you can make it using a stock cube or stock powder)

1 bay leaf

2 tbsp mascarpone cheese

1 handful fresh basil leaves

Salt and pepper

2 tbsp fresh cream

1 Peel and chop the onion into small pieces. Take a big saucepan and cook the onions in the olive oil until they are soft. Add the chopped tomatoes, the sugar, and the liquid stock. Drop in the bay leaf and let everything cook gently for 15 minutes. Take the pan off the heat and add the mascarpone and basil leaves.

2 Pour into a blender and whizz the soup until it is smooth. Taste the soup and season it with some salt and pepper. Pour the soup into bowls and serve with a little swirl of cream poured on top.

Cheesy Corn Triangles

Quick to make and easy to bake, these cheesy
corn triangles are super with soup.

²/₃ cup all-purpose flour
²/₃ cup semolina
1 tbsp baking powder
¹/₂ cup milk
2 eggs, beaten
¹/₄ cup butter
¹/₂ cup sweetcorn
1 cup grated cheese
Salt and black pepper

Set the oven to 350°F. Always ask a
grown-up to help with the oven.
Lightly grease an 18-cm square
cake pan.

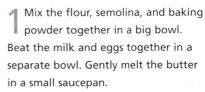

1 Mix the flour, semolina, and baking
powder together in a big bowl.
Beat the milk and eggs together in a
separate bowl. Gently melt the butter
in a small saucepan.

2 Add the sweetcorn and cheese to
the flour mixture, then pour in the
eggy mixture and add the butter.

3 Give the ingredients in the bowl a good stir to mix them thoroughly.

5 Smooth the top and bake for 20 minutes until golden brown and springy to the touch. Cut into triangles and serve straight away.

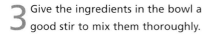

4 Spoon the mixture into the pan.

Easy-Peasy Pizz

These simple pizzas are not only easy to
they taste brilliant too!

For four people:

3 tbsp olive oil

1 large onion, peeled and
finely chopped

1 clove garlic, crushed

14oz tin chopped tomatoes

1 tsp superfine sugar

Salt and pepper

Generous handful of fresh basil

4 English muffins

2 cups Mozzarella cheese, grated

8 mushrooms

2 slices ham

Dried oregano

Set the oven to 350°F. Always ask a
grown-up to help with the oven.

1 Put the onion and garlic into a pan
over a gentle heat and cook until
soft. Add the tomatoes and the sugar.
Let the mixture bubble for 10 minutes
until it thickens and then add salt and
pepper and lots of freshly torn basil.
Remove the mixture from the heat.

2 Cut the muffins in half and lay them on a baking sheet. Spread a little of the tomato sauce over each muffin and sprinkle over the cheese.

3 You can add some mushrooms or ham, or whatever your favorite topping is. Sprinkle over some dried oregano and drizzle with a little olive oil. Bake for 5 minutes, until the cheese is golden brown and bubbling.

Dreamy Creamy Cheese

Did you know that it's easy to make your very own cheese at home – just from a carton of lovely thick Greek yogurt? Well, here's how…

You will need

1 square of cheesecloth or a clean kitchen towel, a sieve, and a medium sized bowl

2 cups Greek yogurt

Salt

Simply take the cheesecloth, lay it in the sieve and set the sieve over the bowl. Pour in the Greek yogurt and refrigerate for about 4 hours. You could leave it overnight if it's easier. The very watery liquid (called the whey) will drain through the sieve, and the yogurt will be transformed into a lovely, thick cheese. Stir in a pinch of salt – and it's ready.

Easy Cheesy Chive Dip

1 quantity homemade cheese (see last recipe)

1 tbsp finely chopped chives

1 clove garlic, crushed

Simply mix everything together in a bowl and give it a good stir.

On the next page are some suggestions to go with your Easy Cheesy Chive Dip.

Mini Sausage and Apricot Dunkers

6 ripe, firm apricots

18 ready cooked mini sausages

6 small wooden skewers

Cut the apricots in half and take out the stone. Cut each apricot into six lengthways. Thread three sausages onto each skewer, with a piece of apricot between each sausage.

Veggie Batons

Choose an assortment of your favorite raw vegetables, such as celery, carrot, cucumber, cauliflower, or cherry tomatoes and carefully wash them. Cut the celery stalks, carrot, and cucumber into thin sticks. Break the cauliflower into small florets and cut the tomatoes in half. Arrange the vegetables around a bowl of Easy Cheesy Chive Dip. The tomatoes are easier to dip if they are put on toothpicks.

Garlicky Tortilla Chips

1 clove garlic, crushed

2 tbsp butter

3 small flour tortillas

$1/2$ tsp paprika

Set the oven to 350°F. Always ask a grown-up to help with the oven.

Beat the garlic and butter together in a bowl and spread it all over one side of the tortillas. Sprinkle over a little paprika and lay them on a large baking sheet. Bake for 5-10 minutes until golden brown. They will turn crunchy as they cool down. Break them into pieces and dunk them into your dip.

Sticky-Licky Chicken with P'Nutty Dip

These are really yummy. Watch out though as grown-ups like them a lot too!

For four people:

2 tbsp brown sugar
1 tbsp sweet soy sauce
1 tbsp olive oil
Juice from $1/2$ a lime
8 chicken mini fillets
8 wooden skewers

1 Stir the sugar, soy sauce, oil, and lime juice together in a bowl. Then carefully thread the chicken fillets onto the wooden skewers.

2 Pour the mixture over the chicken and leave it for half an hour if possible. Broil for 6-8 minutes until cooked, depending on the thickness of the chicken. You will need to turn the chicken over several times during the cooking.

For the dip:

2 tbsp coconut milk

4 tbsp peanut butter

2 tbsp soy sauce

4 tbsp Greek yogurt

Paprika, to garnish

3 To make the dip, simply stir all the ingredients together until well mixed, turn into a pretty bowl and garnish with a sprinkling of paprika.

Pasta 'n' Cheese with Ham 'n' Peas

Pasta makes you go faster, and that's a fact – how many Italian snails do you know?

For four people:

3 cups pasta spirals

1 clove garlic, crushed

3 tbsp mascarpone cheese

3 tbsp milk

3/4 cup cooked ham

8 cherry tomatoes

2 cups cooked peas

1 tbsp finely chopped chives

Salt and pepper

1 Take a big pan of water and add a good teaspoonful of salt. Bring it to the boil and add the pasta (follow the instructions on the packet to see how long to cook it for).

2 While that's cooking, add the crushed garlic to the mascarpone and milk and stir.

3 When the pasta is cooked, drain it and stir in the mascarpone mixture. Tear the ham into pieces, cut the tomatoes in half, and toss it all into the pasta with the cooked peas. Stir in the chives, season with a little salt and pepper and serve at once.

tortellini~ravioli~spaghetti~cannelloni~

Italian Bread

Making bread is great fun, but if you want to make it extra special and super-delicious, just add some chopped herbs and some olive oil and you have Italian bread! Fantastico!

$^1/_2$oz fresh yeast
1 tsp sugar
3 $^1/_2$ cups all-purpose flour
1 tsp salt
3 tbsp olive oil
1-2 tbsp fresh rosemary, finely chopped
1 tbsp fresh thyme leaves, finely chopped

1 Crumble the yeast into a large bowl and stir in the sugar; it will turn soft and creamy. Stir in $^1/_4$ cup warm water. Cover the bowl with a clean kitchen towel and leave it for 10 minutes, until the mixture starts to bubble.

2 In another large bowl, sieve the flour and salt together. Make a hole in the center of the flour and slowly pour in the yeast liquid. Stir the mixture and then pour in 1 cup warm water and a tablespoonful of olive oil.

3 Mix everything to a dough, tip it out onto a floured work surface and knead the dough for 5 minutes, until it feels really soft and springy and is nice and smooth. Leave it in a warm place to rise for about one hour.

Set the oven to 440° F. Always ask a grown-up to help with the oven.

4 When the dough has doubled in size, knead it again for another couple of minutes. Flatten the dough out into an oval or oblong shape about 1in thick, place it on an oiled baking sheet and press your fingers into it to leave little holes everywhere. Drizzle over the remaining olive oil and sprinkle with the chopped herbs. Bake in the oven for 15-20 minutes until golden brown and the bread sounds hollow when tapped on the bottom (you'll need an adult to help with this stage as the bread will be very hot).

Hedgehog Rolls

Makes 12

1 quantity basic bread dough

1 egg, beaten

Raisins, for eyes

Make up the basic bread mix as on page 26, but leave out the herbs. Heat the oven as on page 27. Form the mixture into 12 oval shapes. Using a pair of scissors, make little snips all over the rolls, leaving one end plain (for the face). Place them onto a greased baking sheet, brush with a little beaten egg and leave for 30 minutes to rise again. Push three raisins into the face to act as eyes and nose. Bake for about 10 minutes, until they are golden brown and sound hollow when tapped on the bottom.

Breadsticks

Makes 18
1/2 quantity basic bread dough

Form the mixture into about 18 pieces, each about the size of a walnut. Roll the mixture into long thin snakes. Pop them onto a greased baking sheet and bake for 5-6 minutes, until they are golden brown.

Aunt   Peggy's Eggy Wedges

Auntie Peggy   Wedges are just like a really
delicious quiche, but without the pastry – so
they're super quick to make and super tasting too!

For 4 people:

5 eggs

1 tbsp chives

Salt and pepper

1 tbsp butter

5-6 small florets broccoli, lightly
   cooked

2 tbsp sweetcorn

$1^1/_2$ cups Cheddar cheese,
   grated

Set the oven to 350°F. You'll need an
adult to help with the oven.

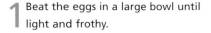

1 Beat the eggs in a large bowl until
  light and frothy.

2 Stir in the chopped chives and
  season with some salt and pepper.

3 Use the butter to grease a non-stick round dish with a 8in diameter. Scatter the broccoli evenly over the base of the dish. Sprinkle over the sweetcorn and two-thirds of the cheese.

4 Carefully pour the egg mixture evenly over the vegetables. Sprinkle with the remaining cheese. Cook for about 20 minutes, until golden and set.

Serve hot or cold, cut into thick wedges.

Nippy Noodles

Great fun to eat with chopsticks!

For four people:

1 thumb-sized knob of ginger
1 clove garlic, crushed
4 tbsp dark soy sauce
1 tsp cornstarch
1 carrot
1 stick celery
4 scallions
1 red bell pepper
3-4 broccoli florets
2 tbsp olive oil

5oz sugar snap peas

$1^1/4$ cups 'straight to wok' noodles

6oz cooked shrimp

1 Peel and grate the ginger and mix it in a bowl with the garlic and soy sauce. Stir in the cornstarch and set the mixture to one side.

2 Peel the carrot. Wash the vegetables and cut the carrot, celery, and red pepper into thin slices. Cut the scallions into short lengths and break the broccoli into very small florets.

3 With an adult to help you, heat the oil in a wok or a big skillet and add the carrots. Cook them for about 2 minutes. Add the remaining vegetables. Cook for 2-3 minutes more.

4 Stir in the soy sauce mixture and the noodles and cook for a further 2 minutes. Finally, add the shrimp, allow them to heat through and then serve straight away.

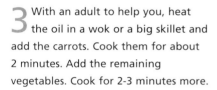

Wild West Ribs

These are real tasty, sticky ribs – brilliant with potato wedges and baked beans!

For four people:

4 tbsp sweet soy sauce

2 tbsp tomato catsup

2 cloves garlic, crushed

8 pork ribs

2 tbsp olive oil

1 Mix the soy sauce and catsup together with the crushed garlic.

2 Lay the ribs in a single layer in an ovenproof dish and spoon the mixture all over them. Leave for half an hour or so if you can.

3 Set the oven to 350°C. Drizzle the ribs with the oil and cook for about 30 minutes. Ask an adult to help turn them over halfway through and baste them with the spare juices.

Funky Fish Cakes

These are great served with tomato catsup!

For 8 fish cakes you will need:

1lb potatoes

$^1/_4$ cup butter

1 egg yolk

$^1/_2$ cup all-purpose flour

7oz can tuna, drained

2 cups fresh or frozen sweetcorn, cooked

1 bunch scallions, trimmed and chopped

Salt and pepper

3 cups breadcrumbs

1 egg, beaten

Sunflower oil for frying

1 Peel the potatoes and cook them in a big pan of boiling, salted water until soft. Add the butter and mash them well, taking care not to leave any lumpy bits! Stir in the egg yolk and the flour.

2 Put the tuna, sweetcorn and scallions into a big bowl and add the potato mixture. Give everything a good stir and season it with some salt and black pepper.

3 Form the mixture into eight ovals and then pinch the fish cake at one end to make a tail, so you have a fish shape. Pop them into the refrigerator and allow the cakes to chill and firm up for 30 minutes or so.

4 Put the breadcrumbs onto a flat surface or big plate. Dip the fish cakes into the beaten egg and then into the breadcrumbs until they are covered completely. Carefully fry the fish cakes in sunflower oil for 3-4 minutes on each side until golden brown.

Fairy Cakes

Everyone loves fairy cakes – not only the fairies!

For 12 fairy cakes:

$^1/_2$ cup softened butter

$^2/_3$ cup superfine sugar

2 eggs

$^3/_4$ cup cake flour

1 tsp baking powder

2 tbsp milk

Set the oven to 350°F. Always ask
an adult to help with the oven.
Fill a fairy cake pan with 12
paper cases.

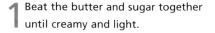

1 Beat the butter and sugar together
until creamy and light.

2 Carefully add one egg and stir it in
until the mixture is smooth. Do the
same with the second egg.

3 Sieve the flour and baking powder into the mixture in the bowl.

4 Add the milk and beat everything together until smooth.

5 Drop a big spoonful of the mixture into each paper case. Cook for 15-20 minutes, until the cakes feel springy when pressed lightly with a finger. Leave them to cool slightly in the pan, then lift them out onto a wire cooling rack.

Cake Icing

Vanilla Buttercream

$1/2$ cup softened butter

$1^1/2$ cups confectioners' sugar

2-3 drops vanilla extract

2 tbsp milk

Runny Glacé Icing

$1/2$ cup confectioners' sugar

1-2 tbsp warm water

Sieve the confectioners' sugar to get all the lumps out and then mix it with the water until it is thin enough to spread, but not too runny. For a lemony icing, use lemon juice instead of water.

To make buttercream, place the softened butter into a bowl and sieve the confectioners' sugar into it. Add the vanilla extract and milk and beat everything together until smooth. Use it to decorate fairy cakes and sponge cakes.

Have fun choosing a variety of sweet and colorful decorations to finish off your fairy cakes.

Fairy Cake Variations

Butterfly Cakes

Cut a small piece of cake from the top of each cake and cut the slice into two to make the butterfly wings. Place a blob of buttercream in the hole and then pop two wings back onto each cake. Sprinkle with confectioners' sugar.

Father Christmas

Use red ready-to-roll icing to make a hat and runny icing for the beard, eyes, nose, and mouth.

Spider

Use chocolate buttercream for the body and thin chocolate sticks for legs.

Teddy Bear

Use chocolate buttercream with white and milk chocolate buttons for nose and ears.

Lion

Melt a small bar of caramel chocolate and add to vanilla buttercream. Use it to make a lion's face and mane.

Flowers

Use ready-made icing flowers.

Cows

Use ready-to-roll icing and make animal shapes, then stick onto cake with runny icing.

Clowns

Use bought decorations and silver dragee balls around edges.

-Licking Lemon Pie

pie and twice as nice!

2 cups digestive biscuits

$1/4$ cup butter

2 cups mascarpone cheese

6fl oz tin condensed milk

2 juicy lemons

Fresh fruit or curly chocolate
shavings, to decorate

You will need a round 8in shallow
loose-bottomed pan.

2 Melt the butter in small saucepan
and then pour over the biscuit
crumbs and mix. Press evenly into the
pan and leave to set in the refrigerator.

1 Put the biscuits into a strong plastic
bag and bash them with a rolling
pin until they look like breadcrumbs.
Tip into a mixing bowl.

3 Put the mascarpone and condensed
milk into a large bowl. Carefully
grate the lemons and add the zest,
then squeeze in the juice as well.

4 Beat everything together until the mixture is smooth and thick, then spread it over the biscuit base and chill in the refrigerator for an hour.

5 Decorate the top with fresh fruit or make curly chocolate shavings by scraping a bar of chocolate with a vegetable peeler.

Trifle Towers

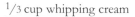

You can use raspberries instead of ~~berries~~ to make these fruity delicious trifles – or use ~~a mixture~~ of both. They look nicest of all in tall sundae glasses.

To make 4:

4 fairy cakes

2 tsp strawberry preserve

2 tbsp strawberry cordial

2 1/2 cups strawberries

1 carton custard sauce
  (about 1 1/2 cups)

1/3 cup whipping cream

Chocolate flakes or
  sprinklies, to decorate

1 Cut the fairy cakes in half and sandwich them together with the preserve.

2 Cut them into four and place the pieces at the bottom of each of the four glasses. Drizzle some strawberry cordial over the sponge pieces to moisten them. Cut the strawberries into quarters and divide them between the glasses, covering the sponge. Pour over a layer of custard.

3 Whip the cream in a mixing bowl until it is thick.

4 Place a spoonful of whipped cream on top of the custard.

5 Decorate with chocolate flakes and sprinklies and pop them in the refrigerator until you are ready to eat them.

SH
B

Strawberry Skewers

Strawberries and chocolate – yum!
Food doesn't get much better!

To make 8 skewers you will need:

5oz white chocolate

24 strawberries

8 physalis* or grapes

Small skewers

*Physalis are pretty golden berries that are covered in a thin lacy husk. Sometimes they are called Chinese lanterns because that is exactly what they resemble. They are also known as Cape gooseberries and can be bought at supermarkets and good greengrocers.

Melt the chocolate in a bowl over a pan of gently simmering water and then remove it from the heat. Carefully dip the bottom of the strawberries into the chocolate, one at a time and then lay them onto a clean plate to set. When all the strawberries are set, gently thread three onto each skewer and push a physalis or grape on to the end of each one. Keep them cool until it's time to eat them.

Candy Strings

A necklace of your favorite candies that looks great and tastes good too! They are such fun to make as a party game.

You will need:

A darning needle or fairly large needle

Some shirring elastic

A selection of candies, such as marshmallows, jellies, cereal hoops, etc

Pass the shirring elastic through the eye of the needle (if you have a darning needle, this should be quite easy). Thread a selection of your favorite candies and cereals onto it, then tie a knot in it to join it up into a necklace and wear it until you want to eat it!

Little Apple Tarts

These apple tarts are so crisp and light and lovely to eat – no one will ever know just how quick and simple they are to make!

To make 12:

2 sheets filo pastry

2 tbsp butter, melted

2 medium cooking apples

4 tbsp superfine sugar

Confectioners' sugar, to sprinkle

Set the oven to 350°F. Always ask an adult to help with the oven.You will need a 12-cup mini muffin pan.

2 Lay two squares together, one on top of the other, and press them gently into the mini muffin pan to make little tartlet cases. Bake for 3-4 minutes until crisp and golden. Leave them to cool on a wire rack.

1 Cut the filo pastry into squares of about 2in and brush them with melted butter.

3 Meanwhile, peel the apples and cut out the cores.

4 Chop the apples into small pieces. Cook them gently in a small saucepan with a spoonful of water for about 5 minutes until they are soft and mushy. Take the pan off the heat and leave them to cool. Mash the apples with a fork and stir in the superfine sugar.

5 Put a spoonful of apple into each filo case; give them a sprinkling of confectioners' sugar and serve at once.

The Chumblies

The Chumblies are a family of crunchy, munchy cookie folk. Make them some funky clothes with runny icing and tubes of edible writing gel.

Makes about 12 depending on the size of cutter used.

1/2 cup butter
3/4 cup all-purpose flour
1/3 cup semolina
1/4 cup superfine sugar
1 cup confectioners' sugar
Tubes of edible writing gel
You will need one or two people-shaped cookie cutters

Set the oven to 300°F. Always ask an adult to help with the oven.

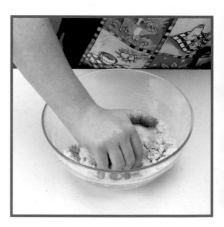

1 Rub the butter and flour together in a bowl with your fingertips until the mixture looks like fine breadcrumbs.

2 Add the semolina and superfine sugar. Squash everything together until you have a ball of firm dough. Sprinkle a bit of flour onto the work surface and roll the dough flat.

3 Using a cookie cutter, cut out your Chumblies and lay them carefully on a baking sheet. Bake for 10 minutes until light golden brown. Leave them to cool on a wire rack. When they are cold, they will be nice and crunchy.

4 Sieve the confectioners' sugar and mix with a little water until you have a spreadable icing that isn't too runny. Use the icing and tubes of edible gel to decorate the biscuits, making a colorful, wacky wardrobe for the Chumblies to wear.

Mini Christmas Puddings

These little treats look so pretty and taste so good –
they're sure to become a Christmas favorite!

15 digestive biscuits

5oz semi-sweet chocolate

$^1/_4$ cup butter

3 tbsp golden syrup

6 glacé cherries, quartered

$^1/_4$ cup raisins

Yellow, green, and red ready-to-roll
  icing, to decorate

2 Melt the chocolate, butter and
golden syrup together in a bowl
over a pan of gently simmering water.

1 Put the biscuits into a strong plastic
bag and bash them with a rolling
pin until they look like fine
breadcrumbs.

3 Pour the chocolate mixture into a
bowl and stir in the biscuit crumbs,
cherries and raisins.

4 Form the mixture into small balls and refrigerate them on a plate to set for half an hour or so.

5 Decorate the tops using yellow ready-to roll-icing to make the custard sauce, green to make holly shapes, and red to make small berries.

Tutti-frutti Popsicles

You can use plastic molds bought from kitchen equipment stores to make great popsicles at home, but I like to use clean, empty fromage frais cartons. All these recipes make 6.

You will need wooden popsicle sticks – these can be bought quite easily from good kitchen stores. Halfway through the freezing time, simply push the popsicle sticks down into the molds and return them to the freezer until frozen.

Papayapops

2 large papayas

Juice of half a lime

3 tsp superfine sugar

Purée the papayas in a blender. Stir in the lime juice and sugar. Pour into the molds and freeze.

Luscious Lemonpops

1 1/2 cups Greek yogurt

3 tbsp lemon curd

Beat the yogurt and lemon curd together, pour the mixture into the molds and freeze.

Strawberry Fizzpops

1/2 cup strawberry cordial

1 cup fizzy mineral water

Mix the cordial and water together, pour into the molds and freeze.

Mangopops

1 large ripe mango

1 1/2 cups Greek yogurt

Squeeze of lime juice

Purée the mango flesh in a blender. Stir in the yogurt and lime juice, pour into the molds and freeze.

Lemonade Fizzypops

1 1/2 cups lemonade made with real lemons

Pour into the molds and freeze.

Milkypops

2/3 cup heavy cream

1/3 cup condensed milk

1/4 cup whole milk

3-4 drops vanilla extract

Sprinklies, to decorate

Whip the cream until thick. Fold in the condensed milk and then carefully stir in the milk and vanilla extract. Pour into the molds and freeze. When the popsicles are frozen, turn them out of the molds and roll them in sprinklies.

Orange Fruitypops

1 1/2 cups fresh orange juice

Pour the orange juice into the molds and freeze.

Mintypops

3/4 cup mascarpone cheese

1 cup whole milk

1 tbsp sugar

8 mint chocolate sticks, chopped into small pieces

Whizz everything together in a blender until smooth, pour into the molds and freeze. For an extra treat, dip the ends into cooled melted chocolate.

Chewy Chocolate
Cherry Bite

This lovely, easy-to-make chocola___ ___dge would make a
very special present for someone. ___k it into
a pretty box and tie with ribbon.

7oz semi-sweet chocolate
$1/4$ cup butter
1 tbsp cocoa powder
$1/5$ cup heavy cream
$2^1/2$ cups confectioners' sugar
8 glacé cherries

1 Put the chocolate, butter and cocoa in a bowl over a
pan of gently simmering water until the chocolate is
melted. Stir everything together, pour into a mixing bowl
and add the cream. Beat in the confectioners' sugar.

2 Chop the cherries into small pieces and fold them into the mixture.

3 Spoon the mixture into a shallow cake pan and smooth the top. Chill in the refrigerator until set and then cut into neat squares.

Yummy Chocolate ake

Diday Cake

This is the yummiest, scrummiest chocolate cake you can imagine. Decorate the top with fab things like marshmallows, jelly beans, crumbled chocolate flakes, or any of your favorite candies.

Cake mixture:

$1/2$ cup softened butter

$2/3$ cup superfine sugar

2 eggs

1 cup cake flour

$1^1/2$ tsp baking powder

2 big tbsp cocoa powder

2 tbsp milk

Chocolate buttercream:

$1/2$ cup softened butter

$1^1/2$ cups confectioners' sugar

2 big tbsp cocoa powder

2 tbsp milk

Set the oven to 350°F. Always ask an adult to help with the oven. Then grease two round 7in cake pans.

1 Beat the butter and superfine sugar together until creamy and light. Carefully add one egg and stir it in until the mixture is smooth. Do the same with the second egg.

2 Sieve the flour, baking powder, and the cocoa into the mixture, then add the milk and beat everything together until smooth.

3 Divide the mixture between the two cake pans and gently smooth the tops.

4 Cook for about 20 minutes, until the cakes feel springy when pressed lightly with a finger. Leave them to cool for a short while in the pans and then turn them out onto a wire cooling rack.

5 Now make the buttercream. Place the softened butter into a bowl and sieve the confectioners' sugar and cocoa powder into it. Add the milk and beat everything together until smooth.

6 When the cakes are completely cold, spread half of the buttercream onto one of the cakes, put the other cake on top and spread the remaining buttercream across the top. For an extra special effect, make swirls in the buttercream using the prongs of a fork. Decorate with your favorite candies.

Monkey Business

Not only do bananas taste brilliant – they're packed with goodness too. We all know that monkeys eat lots of bananas – that's how they get the energy for all that monkey business swinging through the trees!

Quick Banana Brûlée

This recipe makes a scrumptious dessert in just a few minutes!

For four people:

4 small ripe bananas

2 cups Greek yogurt

3 tbsp demerara sugar

2 Divide the yogurt between the dishes and smooth the top. Sprinkle over a layer of sugar and broil until golden and bubbling. Leave the brûlées to go cold, but don't put them in the refrigerator. When cold, the tops will be crunchy and caramelized.

1 Peel the bananas and cut them into thin slices. Place a quarter of the bananas into each of four small ramekins or dishes.

Hunny Bunnies

Hunny Bunnies are lovely for breakfast, for snacks and are great with Quick Banana Brûlée.

For four people:

4 slices brioche or white bread
1 tbsp butter
2 tbsp honey

Set the oven to 350°F. Always ask an adult to help with the oven.

1 Butter the brioche or bread slices and spread with honey. Put the slices onto a baking sheet and bake for 10 minutes until golden.

2 Remove them from the oven and cut out bunny shapes. The crusts will be crunchy and yummy – you might like to eat these as you work. That's what we call 'cook's bonus'.

Bananalicious Shakes

for Bag

Try to use really ripe bananas for this – so ripe in fact, that the skins have started to turn black! The flavor of the milkshake will be much better – just try it and see.

For each shake you will need:

1 very ripe banana

2 tsp superfine sugar

1 cup cold milk

2 small scoops vanilla ice cream

Chocolate sprinklies

Put the banana and sugar into a food processor and whizz until you have a smooth purée. Add the milk and one scoop of ice cream and whizz again. Pour the shake into a long glass and add the second scoop of ice cream and the sprinklies.

Spooks' Punch

This is a big bowl of lovely fruity punch, just the right color for blood! Make some ice hands for a funky Halloween party drink.

2 cups still lemonade

2-3 small sized surgical gloves

4 cups cranberry juice

2 cups apple juice

2 cups passionfruit juice

1 Carefully fill the surgical gloves with the lemonade, tie a secure knot in the ends and put them into the freezer overnight (you could just use water if you prefer).

2 When you are ready to serve the Spooks' Punch, pour all the juices into a big glass bowl. Carefully peel away the gloves to leave really cool ice hands! Float them in the punch and serve it straight away.

My Favorite Recipes

When you have tried the recipes in this book, why not experiment with some of them and create your own recipes? Make a note of them here.